COMING ABOUT

COMING ABOUT

Michelle Gillett

Four Way Books
Tribeca

Please direct all inquiries to:
Editorial Office
Four Way Books
POB 535, Village Station
New York, NY 10014
www.fourwaybooks.com

Library of Congress Cataloging-in-Publication Data

Names: Gillett, Michelle, author.
Title: Coming about / Michelle Gillett.
Description: New York, NY : Four Way Books, 2017.
Identifiers: LCCN 2017000676 | ISBN 9781945588006 (pbk. : alk. paper)
Classification: LCC PS3607.I4442 A6 2017 | DDC 811/.6--dc23
LC record available at https://lccn.loc.gov/2017000676

This book is manufactured in the United States of America and printed on acid-free paper.

Four Way Books is a not-for-profit literary press. We are grateful for the assistance
we receive from individual donors, public arts agencies, and private foundations.

This publication is made possible with public funds from the New York State Council on the Arts,
a state agency.

We are a proud member of the Community of Literary Magazines and Presses.

Distributed by University Press of New England
One Court Street, Lebanon, NH 03766

We have remembered your way of looking, never missing a thing.
You gave us that. Looking.

CONTENTS

When Michelle Gillett wrote the poems in *Coming About*, I'm sure she didn't realize it would be a valedictory manuscript. She was too full of vitality and involvement in her myriad family, civic and literary activities, including teaching workshops and writing a regular column for the *Berkshire Eagle*. Even so, these poems are threaded with dread as they sweep you into their powerful emotional vortex, but they acknowledge, as well as accept, whatever comes next.

Michelle was my friend. We met decades ago at Bread Loaf Writers' Conference, both of us bursting with excitement as we shared our love of poems and our dreams of writing them. Over the years we also shared our work, and I was aware of the "pockets of time" that she—and her family before her in World War II—lived through. Those moments are not so much confessional as they are flashes of personal experience that allow her to talk about universal issues. Some poems give you a glimpse into the horrors her English mother and Austrian father experienced before coming to the States, making you feel the brutality and randomness of war and history. But the poems—however much they acknowledge the place of fear and danger in human life—also express tentative acceptance, with the realization that "there is no going back."

Whether the subject is the Holocaust, a summer house, the death of parents, maternal anxiety, gardening, love, or memory, the poems totter between sorrow at the passage of time and finding a way to face the future. That mode may not always be completely hopeful, but she finds ways to avoid despair. As she says in "Elephant Hearts":

> Like anyone who'd give her heart to change
> what cannot be moved, I favor resemblances.

As she examines the various choices she has made, she reminds herself: "it is easy to forget how close / I came to the wrong life." She is also always aware she is leasing, not 'buying,' time. And as she plants 300 daffodil bulbs in the last poem in this volume, she knows she is "planting for a season I can only imagine."

I will always remember my dear, loving friend as a thoughtful, empathic, engaged, and industrious person. And as a powerful poet, to which these poems attest.

Jacquelyn Malone

The Lungfish

Deep down inside, I am afraid of the lungfish
suspended in its tank in the darkened room
meant to emulate time when desert was ocean
and ocean was all there was before we crept
on our stubs from the watery hem of existence
and blinked at undiluted light. There was no
going back although we still lacked breath enough
to inherit the earth. Head down in its gloomy tank,
God's first creature—made in his own image
before we began to feel at home in shallows and muck,
grew legs and arms, sucked in air and named ourselves—
is who we are: bone and gut, God's face before we invented it,
stone-like, wide mouth feeding on every element.

Vespids

It's down. The hornets' nest.
Now first sting of frost on the ground
and we see no threat,
only the hollow where harm lived.
Everything the season housed has flown:
yellow jackets idling low in the grass,
bats fanning the dusk, the hornets
threading close to the roof.
When we were children
we'd leap from our beds,
arms flung wide. In the seconds
before landing, we didn't know fear
resides in gravity or stars fall
into themselves. We imagined rising
over the roofs not like souls
detached from bodies, but as bodies
resisting the world. Light in my hands
when I lifted it from the eave, fervor gone,
no longer wadded in industry, this testament
to vanishings is too fragile to hold.

Not There

As we drive past Benedict Pond, you make me stop the car.
Listen, you say, a loon. But it is only the day
lifting out of its surfaces—yellow lilies
floating on the water, shade occupying the trees,
the kind of clarity that comes when there is no more
to say and we invent other sounds.
What do we need to hear beyond our stories
to make this afternoon singular among the ones that go
so un-oracled they become the same
repeated notes? It is always dangerous to move
deeper into that forest of listening, always easy
to get lost in what is not there. The loon's song
sounds like laughter when it means alarm,
but we imagine happiness—
a mistake we can't help stopping for.

Love Poem 137

This time, the boat we pushed off in
in the first 136 will stay tied to the dock.
No more gliding through corridors of light
watching the bluegills dart.
When we cast our lines, they won't be
filaments of time. All these years,
rowing across this same body of water.
How many poems ago did I watch you
lean and straighten as you pulled the oars?
I won't quote Wordsworth again,
although I love the *underthirst*
and tried to use it in 129.
In poems 84 and 85, a heron weighted the spruce
at the narrow end of the lake. I failed
to make its heaviness a metaphor for love.
The six-point buck we saw swimming across
so many poems ago surprised us
as love sometimes does.
It only got as far as a few lines.
The love poem shifts on its anchor.
Across the lake, in the green cottage, you wait.

How to Resuscitate a Bird

If your bird is not breathing, but still
has a heartbeat, begin rescue breathing.
Remember that mannequin, Annie, her rubber mouth,
her perfect nose, so life-like in her breathlessness?
Hold the bird's head in one hand, support the body in the other.
We practiced holding and releasing
air into her parted lips, where to find her heart and press—
in case a stranger collapses on the street or an elderly aunt
succumbs, one hand to her chest, the turkey on her plate untouched.
Or a child does not rise to the surface, but dangles, halted and blue.
If the bird is small, seal your lips around the beak and nares.
At night, when I listen to my daughters' breath falling like birds
escaping the wind, I try not to think of the boy
who slipped through the railings on the Golden Gate Bridge,
his mother grasping at air. I don't think of the bough breaking
or the nest, its intersecting twigs, lining of feathers and grass.
To adequately inflate the lungs takes practice and some skill.
The smallest thing deserves such hope although it seems ridiculous.
Blow five quick breaths into the bird's beak,
watch for the sternum rising.
A heart can stop for no apparent reason—mid-flight, mid-song,
a loved one fall so suddenly, it takes your breath away.
We were told to shake her gently, ask, "Annie, are you alright?"
And when she didn't answer, we checked her pulse,
put our ear to her lips, began
rescue breathing to survive our helplessness.

Still Time

Before we thought to sell the summer house, give up the view
of sky and lake, before the days grew short and time hurried us
faster than we thought it could, our daughter left for the wrong man.
The wrong man took her money. Showed her the back of his hand,
or was it worse than that?

I sat on the dock and read book after book looking for daughters
in words others wrote: around me birches, hemlocks,
their wavering likenesses. How could I not disturb the surface
when I stepped into the water? What distance is too far to swim?
I was starting to understand stealing a heart,

no going back. "Love," she said, and refused to see the difference
between need and want. Before the perch depleted the trout,
we hung baited traps and kept a count. I counted on the balance.
What would I give up to get a daughter back? What I have faith in,
the warmth, the not yet.

My Family Is Superstitious

Never allow thirteen at the table,
mix red and white flowers,
kill a spider, open an umbrella
indoors. Never cut your nails
on a Friday, walk under a ladder,
put new shoes on a table. If you spill salt,
blame your sister; if a sparrow enters
the house, consider who should die
first in this family with its unfortunate
history of wrong place, wrong time.
The person you pass on the stairs
might not know the bad luck
you pass on while you cross
your heart, rub the rabbit's foot
you carry in your pocket,
stop to touch wood. Do not look
over your shoulder into the devil's eyes.
Swerve to avoid the black cat running
in front of your car to the curb
where three ravens huddle.
Do not leave even a hair of yourself
by the stream where you dip and rinse
slices of broken mirror
to wash out seven years of bad luck.
Look how water distorts the light.
A drowned woman floats face up.

Resettlement

Right after the war, they came—
dark braids full of lice
shorn by our maid in the backyard.
Our mother bought them dresses
with matching cardigans
and lined us up on the steps:
four little girls of her own,
three just passing through.
Squinting at the lens,
she motioned us close to get us all in.

At the train station, they kissed our cheeks,
kept saying, "goodbye."
We let them keep the dolls
we'd lost interest in.
Their mother said she'd write
as soon as they got settled.
We smiled and waved
as if they were our friends.
How soon after they left,
their names escaped us.

Elsewhere

Once there were ships with cargoes of children,
names pinned to their coats. They held small valises
and looked down from the decks.
Only a few toys allowed.
For a holiday, the mothers said, waving from below.

They almost sent me away in the war.
Can you imagine? my sister said.
We were talking about what made us afraid,
what fears we carry still—I imagine her one doll
and two books, her gas mask under her arm.

My sister slept instead at our grandparents' house.
When the buzz bombs flew over and fell
in the field across the road, our mother held her
in her arms in the blacked-out corridor.
In the morning, cows grazed beside failed bombs.

How little I know of near misses,
born in another country on the other side of loss.
When the planes flew over, all the apples fell on the roof.
Fear of abandonment, waking in strange houses, rooms
where darkness is intentional and no one makes a sound.

The Dictionary of Underwater Photography

The book my father wrote probed
the depths of water's language:
Aluminaut, buoyancy, exposure.

For ten cents a word, I copied to index cards
and filed in cardboard boxes taken down
and shelved on Saturdays, terms for how to capture

"the wonders of the ocean floor."
Suspended in boredom, unable to escape,
I chose not to think about that world

where so much light gets lost
in absorption, so much in scattering,
where my father submerged himself

in techniques of visibility while I transcribed:
submersive for the deep, capacity to stay afloat,
waves of light bending as they travel.

Why come back now—Saturday afternoons forfeited
to words I didn't care about, flash
of that distant girl who wanted her own lexicon

for seeing. My father's book ordered words
that penetrate the surface. Of course they must
return like anything forsaken—

synonyms for lost time, distances corrected
swimming up from darkness, my first vocabulary
for vision: angle, focus, light.

Swimming with My Sisters

We go up to our chests, backs to the shore
where umbrellas tilt and gull voices lift.
The horizon blues where boats dissolve.
In the sunlit zone, shadows merge
and minuscule creatures drift—grey-green plankton,
silver lances, the seaweed we call *main de mer.*
We have learned to tread water,
to read movement in the calm. Down the beach
from the lifeguard stand, our mother spreads her towel.
She lights a cigarette and waves. A blue bandana shades her neck.
Soon one of us will wade too far, one stay under too long.
Suspended between crest and draw, we hold our breath.
Waves lift and lower us. Our mother cannot swim.

Robbing the Bees

Murmur of bees in goldenrod
beside the north field path, almost inaudible
like voices in the psychiatric hospital
where I worked years ago—doors
closed on the unsayable. Everyone listening
for words to slip through. Lorna would lock herself
in the utility closet to have it out with her selves.
Bill could hear the squirrels chew.
Patients with day-night reversal whispered
in their rooms. From his portrait
by the main entrance, Freud's eyes followed
you through the room. A nurse said to me once,
"If these walls could talk..."
and if they could, they would wait
until the doctors went home,
the receptionist locked her knitting in a drawer,
the night staff finished dispensing pills.
Then the walls would start spilling
from plaster and studs, years of stored secrets,
seductions, truths, and talk all night
about what escapes notice, what we keep to ourselves.

Dead Man's Float

for my father

Forever it seems, he would lie there—
sun glossing his back, his tanned bald head
lotion-slick, face down in the salt water pool,
arms and legs outstretched,
July afternoon boxed in turquoise cement,
black tile numbers measuring depth.
Told to count the seconds he floated
motionless, water-deaf, we sat,
legs dangling over the edge.
It was all we could do
not to reach for him, to shout him back.
The dead man was pretend—
he was teaching us to swim,
the water holding him
the same way memory does:
nudging him forward,
drifting him back,
How he startled us when he rose laughing,
"See how easy it is."
Light streams down his face before
he holds his invisible breath
and lies down in the water again.

"This Is the Final Day of Years of Sweetness"

Petrarch 314

Wormwood. Eyesore. The orchard trees no longer cared for.
Still we pick up windfalls, pull spotted fruit from branches,
take them home to boil down, counting on the flavor—sweetest
at season's end like the changes we've outlived.
One death after another. Our parents keep
their distance now—ashes tended by stone.

We slipped the rings from their fingers, bands of stones—
a diamond, two sapphires—and begin to take for
granted days without bad news. This is the first we have lived
in abundance. This is what absence bestows. Sun rakes the hills, branches
fill with sky. It's almost too much. The earth's sweet
insistence steadies us when we walk the path that keeps

us fixed to the world like a finger on the book keeping
the page when we look away—we are only a stone's
throw from losing our place now that the stories are told. Sweeter
yet: apples cooking, time stopping over the house. Before
long, deer will come out of the woods, shift under branches
to eat windfalls we left. Nothing we said can be taken back. We live

unencumbered by guilt. Her skin turned livid,
his eyes wouldn't close. We don't mind that they keep
to themselves. Soon the rest of the leaves will fall from branches;
Later today, rain changing to snow. The stone
sundial in the garden keeps time by shadows. By four
o'clock, it's nearly dark. My sister stirs the pot. "Is it sweet

enough?" she wants to know. We like it tart, just a little sweet.
She passes me the spoon. We've had our taste of final days, life-
less hands against our lips, one last kiss before

the cold takes hold. Memory stores them for us—death's keep-
sakes like November's final offerings: stones
on the path—mica flecked, dry husks, spiked rosettes, the twisted branches'

lichen. There is always more to gather, branching
past season's end. I learned the dead are not sweet-
tempered. Refusing to answer, to look at our faces—stony-
hearted, they ignore our voices. When they were alive
they said they loved us. Now we keep
to ourselves a happiness we did not know before

they left—broken like branches, distinct from their bodies, living
our lives without them. Grief can be forfeited. Nothing's worth keeping
as much as this sweetness where each day is the next to the last one.

Ghazal

What dream was lost when the fox's cry broke into the dark
calling his mate across the field and woke me to the dark?

No one speaks the language anymore, those who escaped
blamed hunger or weather when they spoke of the dark.

One summer, we traveled from country to country.
High on the mountain, village men stoked fires in the dark.

Only a thin pane between us and the frozen world—
the cold carries the smell of wood smoke in the dark.

Remember Audrey Hepburn in "Wait Until Dark,"
smashing the lights, making a deadly joke of the dark?

What faith we have in sleep, trusting our bodies will wake
while night fills our vacancies—shadow-strokes in the dark.

"Time hurries by and we're here and we're gone," warns the song.
Someone used to whisper my name and hold me in the dark.

Bear

The neighbor is trying to sail a kite
but it lifts no higher than the fence;
still his children cheer and laugh.
What matters is possibility, after all it's spring,
everything attempting to rise.
A few mosquitoes, newly hatched, speck the air,
hunger propelling them like the bear I saw last night
from the bedroom window, incongruent
in my suburban yard, pulling the feeder down,
scooping up seed. He rocked the split rail fence
climbing over, then ambled away—fluid and lithe

as a fat man who is light on his feet
like the one who waltzed with me at my sister's wedding,
suit jacket gaping, his paw on my back
guiding me as if I too could dance in my first
pair of heels, my daisy crown and yellow dress.
Black bears are shy, rarely dangerous. Who else
would lead me to the floor? It could have been *Moonlight*
Serenade or one of those songs we hum now and then,
surprising ourselves with memory, something familiar
exciting the dark, drawing us near.

Parrot's Lament

(from Sappho, Fragment 30)

No more than the bird with piercing voice,
I don't sing or speak. Although my owner
slows his syntax, whistling and coaxing me,
I am a failure at mimicry.

I had a companion once—she escaped
from the hooded cage. I could hear her
hesitation, then her flailing at the walls.
I don't want to leave.

I have my mirror and my bell,
my cuttlebone, the swing.
He fills the little water trough, puts down
shredded paper, hangs the bough of seed.

Sometimes the mirror gives me back
the shape of my exertions. I hang and preen.
I would like to please him more—
force consonants between my tongue and beak,

work the vowels up my throat to say
what he repeats. But how would he distinguish
truth from mockery? Sometimes he lifts me out
to perch on his index finger, his voice all I need.

We Inherit the House

Goldenrod invades the beds; bees haze the yellow clusters.
She knelt here once, yanked the stubborn roots,
called me from the house to stake the asters.
We tied them to poles with strips of nylons.
Behind glass doors: china shepherdess, stereopticon.
Piano rolls turned out *Summertime,*
By the Light of the Silvery Moon.
Rainbow trout on the counter, slit from tail to throat,
lettuce rinsed in the colander, the table set for company,
delphiniums in the porcelain vase.

She swam early mornings, towel hung on a birch limb,
the water smudged with mist. Of course, we kept the photographs
but what would we want with her evening clothes—
clutches sequined and pearled, moth-chewed wraps?
Before she died, she would sit by the lake, reading a book,
her mind already losing its place. No good to us,
the finger bowls and miniatures, the buttons saved in jars.
Spectral as our faces in the window,
the past makes way for the next accumulation.
Someone touches the piano keys; someone raises a glass.

Elephant Hearts

Unlovely fruit, mottled brown, too big
to fit my palm. I dropped into a bag
half a dozen to take home, let ripen in the blue Spode bowl.

I bought them for their name: muscle of those mammals
that circle their loved ones' remains
and caress tusk and bone.

Like anyone who'd give her heart to change
what cannot be moved, I favor resemblances:
plums to animal,

how hunger comes close to patience.
Each time I press for softness, I expect resistance.
You bring me dahlia tubers dug up from your garden—

dusty fists of swollen thumbs, sprouting eyes
that will grow into pale pink blooms named *Bliss*—
what I want from happiness but cannot hold.

Instead of my heart, I give you plums.
When ripe, cut them toward the center,
pull flesh away from stone.

Given Time

Light dying down the stems, late afternoons like this,
"The garden is haunting," you say. And the stems,
clustered with blooms, hold nothing back—
asters and phlox bow down with purple and pink.
None of them last if picked, which is why we stay
walking the length of the beds, naming what we can:
anenome, lamium, the dinner plate dahlia
I lift to see where the petals begin
radiating plum to amethyst, knowing the wish to possess
what I love is not the same as permission. It takes restraint
not to cut the stems, snip some stalks
of coreopsis. But they would droop
within the hour, dust the mantel yellow.
This is what I have to go on:
long shadows cooling the earth.

Apologia

I have always been sorry.
Blame it on the war, my widowed mother.
The great-aunts the Nazis marched to the river,
shot in the back, floated face down
in the current. Forgive me
my trespasses, especially in the arms
of men married to women I know.
Clumps of witch grass yanked from the bed
where I've planted lilies and daffodils
accept my apologies as do the roses I dig up,
even the ones with new leaves. Too much dead
wood, too much shade from the trees. How wrong
I am more often than not, I am sorry for that
and for not being happier. After all it is spring,
everything atoned for. Please excuse the secrets
I carry like these thorny canes to the burn pile,
carefully, so they don't stab my skin.
You who allow my indulgence in regret,
how merciful you are, reading the paper,
looking up now and then to survey the yard—
green lawn, maple tree, border
of astilbe and ferns, content with your lot,
nothing between you and your past.

Hemlock

The bolt struck the roots, corkscrewed up
the trunk, blasting off long swags of bark,
baring smooth pink wood where it breathes,
fills with sap, would heal if human,
could be triaged or appeal to God.
Mortally wounded, the arborist said,
has to come down before it falls on the house.
The house holds its usual assurances—
corridors branch to rooms; walls mirror
the bending sprays, grow at night
so shadow-scraped, we pray to dark and light
and try not to think about waking
grounded in brightness,
without limbs to break us from sky.

Summer House Ledger

Little black book purchased to record
what is broken, needs replacing, is about to
fall apart. My sister notes a robin's nest over the front door.
Bit by bit, the bird arranged her future
the way we dream our human one.
All summer, we enter reparations.
Closet light cord, canoe paddle split in two.
We haven't registered sadness yet,
though the eggs in the nest are doomed by departures
and my sister transplants lilies-of-the-valley
certain they will come back next year, spread
beneath the laurels. They ought to know
better—mother bird at the hub
of screen door traffic, woman kneeling in the dirt,
thinking she has another summer left.

Barred Owl

Don't think he doesn't know you're there—
asleep in the cottage on Inner Road
as he delivers packets of mouse and finch
along the gravel drive, slick fur and feather,
indigestible tail and bone—for you to discover
in the morning when you go out to walk the dogs.
He leaves them for you, waking
to his *hoo-hoo* so close to the window
beside the bed. Bird of prey calling you out,
stalking the smallest shadows. He swallows
them whole, the way you tried
to swallow grief, father, mother
dying in turns, and after them, the sister who
asked for songs: all night rubbing her back,
half-remembering words to *Night and Day, Blue Moon.*
His repeated notes trouble your soul—
you who are nothing but gristle and gut,
cannot thrive on darkness.

Crows

They take possession of the garden, loiter
beneath the birdfeeder, perch on backs
of wrought iron chairs. When the sky darkens,
they assemble in the hemlocks' topmost branches.
flapping and vexing the air. They are watching
for snow, for the fox to crawl past the fence,
for the dogs to run in circles in the yard.
They make a racket as if there were news
beyond shadows falling. I could bang pots and shout
but crows have seventeen calls for warning.
They would gather more forces, not let up
until I brought them the keys to the house,
my strand of pearls. They arrive in threes—
this one near the steps twitches its wings
watching me switch on lamps and pull the curtains closed.

Timing is everything,

I thought as I reached
the top step a few yards from the door
to the patients' residence just below the round window.
First the sound of breaking, then glass
flying down, hitting the marble stoop, spraying the stone
urns; geranium leaves holding slivers; spikes of dracaena
sliced with light; then I looked up and saw him
leaning out, the boy coming down
from meth, soft blond hair to his shoulders—
the one who sits on the couch near the desk
where visitors sign in and out, playing his guitar.
Then he disappeared, yanked away by a nurse.
It was like when you go back to the house
because you forgot your keys and realize the delay
gave just enough distance from
the accident which must have occurred
at exactly the time it would have been you
on the stretcher being fed into
the ambulance beside the crumpled blue
car. Caught in the blind spot,
the unseen comes at you. Even if he fell,
I couldn't have caught him:
boy with arms and legs outstretched,
glass shimmering at my feet.

As the Crow Flies

for J.M.

not straight but curving over the fields
where we walked against the wind, heads bent
like women on a pilgrimage leading to salvation
instead of two friends defying winter weather.
Where ice ridged the path, we went single-file;
behind me, you stopped to catch your breath.
"It's the wind," you said when I turned
as if it were that straightforward.
Instead something veering off course
made you lean against the pasture fence
and lift your hand to your mouth.
The cold cut the story short. Your heart,
your new medication, new precautions.
I'd always followed you, your words
essential to my lexicon. Crows dipped like kites
then settled in the orchard, cawing
as we went by. I didn't want to know
more than you told me. The wind sufficed.

Anatomy

You could be excused
if it made you queasy—not
just the smell
but touching the scalpel to skin,
scissoring through layers
of muscle and fat,
staring at the pebble-
sized heart, the yellow
intestines. But in tenth grade,
I knew I could learn
from the frog

and the following year
from the rat I tacked down
with long silver pins,
stretched to the edges
of the pan. Its body
closed like a curtain until
I slid it open, plucked out
organs, cut paper thin
sections to fit under the lens,

and the fetal pig
in college lab, Fridays at 4.
While my boyfriend waited
in the library, I turned back
flaps of dead skin, exposed
liver and lungs, measured
minutes until I could go to him.
Mine was female. I remember
the bean-shaped ovaries,

the coiled Fallopian tubes.
I traced tube to uterus,
uterus to vagina, labeled
the diagram, handed it in;
formaldehyde-scented,
I escaped to love,

and years later, conceived
the meaning of those lessons
when I saw the dark seam
from my navel to pubic bone
no different from the line drawn down
the center of those creatures.
Linea nigra it is called.
No one knows why

it appears but it could mark
the time a woman is about
to come apart.

Persephone at Home

When she comes back,
mopey and silent, picking at food,
thinner than when she lived on nothing
but promises, so much hurts her eyes—the
yellow kitchen, the unburied sky.
She sleeps as though she had forgotten sleep
all those months, cushioned by dust,
nothing to read but names
in books, heat of their leather
on her palms. She calls it fate
when she pulls the shades,
waits by the phone. Nothing's been
sacrificed, she tells them. She's home.
Demeter on the verge of tears,
stirs the copper pot of polenta.
Zeus numb with daughters,
snips the ends of cigars,
places them in the humidor.
All winter they barely touched, unable
to exchange worry for love.
They still blame each other
even though it is spring
with its age-old compromise: rain
for green, green for the mole
burrowing past bulbs it will not eat—
bitter, toxic
narcissus, her favorite flower,
already sending up shoots.

What the Body Doesn't Remember:

falling
the way the horse doesn't remember
me pulling the reins turning his head
shifting my weight so we both
went down instead of into
the stone wall suddenly in the field
or is it the impact the body forgets
shoulder on stone as I rolled
away from the flailing hoofs

or was it falling
for any man who wanted me
even ones I could not get close to
loving unreliable as the body
holding on to what is gone
like the train carrying me to and from
my hometown station speeding past
houses tenements whole neighborhoods
moving through pockets of time
who doesn't remember
the door closing the car ride north
where winter changed what I knew
here trees bend under white
mantles the horses move through
their own breath the pond is black with ice
and it is easy to forget how close
I came to the wrong life

Arrhythmia

April morning, the disturbance of light
in the room, and the light disturbances:
cat scratching the door, newspaper
on the floor, the clock's digital glow,
the dream I have yet
to shake. I feel my heart
turn strange, an unfamiliar fluttering.
"Nothing serious," the doctor said,
but I don't know what it wants
tapping out this new code
while pear blossoms
screen the sky, white on white.
Shouldn't I give it pause—the body
shifting its gait when I still feel
affection for the world?
It will happen soon enough, heart
more out of step each day, the catch
in the morning's pulse once reliable
as my needs: sleep, breath,
the light that stirs me awake.
I place my hand on my chest
to feel the curious beat—like someone
hurrying to find me but when I turn,
there is nothing that will not wait.

Humpback, Deer Isle

It weighs on us all summer—
carcass rotting on the beach,

washed up in winter, already past
stench, skin hanging in stiff flaps

like torn window shades
from hull-high ribs, flukes gone,

tail chewed by gulls and crows,
clumps of seaweed stuck to bone

at odds with what we want to see
from rocks above the cove—

a dark hump breaching, tail slapping the water.
Instead the ruined shape compels us

to stop and stare until it is familiar
as any abandoned house, weather beaten,

worn down, pine shadows crowding out sun
at windows we want to look through

because vacancy is a story we must finish
for ourselves. We guess at what drove it

from its element, left it stranded,
but all we can make of its story

is no more than the little we know.
Skeletal doors frame water and clouds,

the tide clatters stones across the sand
and eddies around the bones.

Rowing from Monhegan to Manana

I leaned into the dinghy's oars, pulling through the brightness,
Indian summer brightness, mute and clear

as if earlier

the portable radio in the lobster shack had not buzzed with bad news
and the lobsterman in his Red Sox cap and faded t-shirt,
painting his buoys as he did every September,
had not beckoned me inside.
Something terrible

has happened, he said.

I moved closer to the words until we were complicit
in the salt-pocked windows, the torn green shade,
the swag of shocking pink buoys, the radio
repeating itself as island light spilled through
the narrow door into the silence we kept

until he returned to his work
and I walked down the path to the beach
where rowboats shouldered each other,
trash smoldered in metal drums and gulls feasted
on corn cobs and lobster shells.

Between Herring Gut and Smutty Nose
rocks cinched the harbor—the ferry blasted its horn
nearing Pemaquid Point. I needed somewhere

to settle the fear that rose with each stretch of oars
threading me like light through strands of water.

But when I climbed the wooden steps to everything abandoned:
signal house, keeper's dwelling, boathouse and bell,
gone too was the sense that anything can keep us.

There was nothing to hold so I crouched low.
Under my palms lichen's rust clung to stone.

Combing the Fields

from *New York Times* articles, July 17-24, 2014

bodies fell from the sky like rags or clumps of ash
akimbo in the wheat field in the sunflowers
in the Queen Anne's Lace, woman in the black sweater
left arm raised as if signaling someone
blood streaming from her face
woman naked except for her black bra
her grey hair mixing with the grass
a man wearing socks but no pants
right arm placed on his stomach as if in repose
two parrots—one of them lifting up its wing as if waving a peacock
a ten-year-old boy in a red t-shirt that read "Don't Panic"
children's playing cards sprinkled over the road
a sticker book a maxi pad a glass bottle of cologne
white slippers a razor eighty children
long white chicken coops in the distance
human-shaped impressions in the grass

Blind Faith

The curled pages with raised dots,
bound in thick sheaves,
heavyweight to hold the embossed marks,
Old Testament and New,
purchased years ago for the blind girl
who came to Bible study group
so she could take her turn
reading the verses, now lie
dusty on the shelf. These days
the good news comes across
the screen, keyboards instruct
fingertips, and God can speak
from the burning bush, Lazarus rise
from the dead, on disks.
Like so much else we used to touch
to understand forgiveness
when miracles were commonplace
and blindness the best
metaphor for justice,
what good is this relic now?
Once I played that game of trust—
bandana over my eyes, one hand
on the shoulder of the person in front,
the leader calling out in the dark:
up, down, root, rock
and we followed him—
a conga line of sightless hikers
feeling our way, believing

we wouldn't fall and when we stopped
and took our blindfolds off
we'd be restored to seeing
the world just as it was.

Blue Christmas

Driving home from the Chinese restaurant,
you tell me your dream about the Eternal Present
where the future is blank and the past
so remote it can't be recollected.
Etta James is singing "O Holy Night"
on the radio, and we sing with her,
"the weary world rejoices."
There is no more childhood magic, instead
we've learned to weigh unhappiness
against our expectations. For those too sad to feel
the holiday spirit, a local church is hosting
a Blue Christmas—
no carols or candles, just a liturgy of solace.
We sing, "Fall on your knees,"
although our minds keep wandering
to the stubble fields and farms
heavy with afternoon grayness.
You turn up the volume when Etta sings in French
because her accent is so awful.
We are trying to trust in joy—if only for the moment.

Morwenstow, North Cornwall

Robert Stephen Hawker of Morwenstow, vicar to smugglers, wreckers, and dissenters of the area from 1834-1874.

A raw September day we trudged across a muddy pasture
to the coastal path. Their haunches branded with numbers,
sheep browsed nearby. We walked through the churchyard
where washed-over corpses were once laid out for burial
to the cliff where wreckers had stood, swinging false lights
to mislead ships onto jagged rocks that tore bodies to gobbets.
The graveyard pitched downhill. Wind-wrenched trees
grew in to stones, their bark host to forgotten souls,
roots tangling with mossy names, dates rubbed invisible.

I stooped to enter Reverend Hawker's hut built into the cliff
where he had sat smoking opium, writing elegies
for the storm-swept dead. Hawker, the guidebook tells us,
wore a pink brimless hat, a yellow horse blanket cassock,
kept a pet pig for company. I liked best that he sat for hours
in his driftwood room, watching mist unpearling

the horizon, clearing Lundy Island. He knew madness
comes and goes and bodies count for nothing
but what lost selves swim away from. This path
remains close to the edge, the book warns.

Shortcut

Wood smoke blurs the houses beyond the school
where children glance from desks to see snow falling.
Those learning to tell time add hours into days.
Some are sounding out words, breaking apart syllables
to make sense of the world growing whiter.
There is more to memorize but the bell rings
and the girl taking the shortcut home with her brother
has already forgotten the names of continents.
Their boot prints are the first impressions
in the trail along the slope where snow erases
roots above the sheen of ice sealing the river.
When she stumbles he can almost reach her
but the ice doesn't hold. For a long time,
the grown-ups find no body. Downstream
from where she fell—her Little Mermaid backpack,
one pink boot. How many days went by?
The children at their desks can see the frozen river.
They are learning present, past and future,
how far things travel, how to count by twos.

Documentary

Why waste bullets on children
when they will suffocate under the weight
of bodies heavy as doors? No one answers
the knocking. The children tap their fingers raw.

The village children drum on saucepans
to drown out the sounds, falling into
rhythms of their own—rat-a-tatting with sticks
to muffle gunshots, beating out screams with spoons.

Some are taken to the grave to walk
across the bodies, packing them down
to make room for the next group of Jews. Under their feet,
a road knuckled and grooved.

One of the few who survived, only five years old,
is in her seventies now, smiling for the camera
against a backdrop of oaks.

I remember the sun was shining.
I remember holding on to the roots.

The Forest Made Itself Burn

Where you kicked leaves
the earth glowed hot
flames had licked the hillside
black we imagined
lightning or match
made the charred swath
the ground feverish
beneath leaf litter and roots
but things decompose flare up
die down spontaneous
as speaking in tongues
still it was mysterious
the blackened slope
fringed by growth
wood fern and asters
in all the myths fire is stolen
the gods take it back
and punish us
a woman with fingers
melted in a flash fire
once served me lunch
my niece in the pink urn
we gave to the ground
so much is accident
we want to save ourselves
when the gods come down
to take what's theirs
they leave us this
faint smell of smoke
untwining over
the dry stream bed

you took my hand crossing
embers smoldering
behind us hidden sparks
we chose not to extinguish

Two-Timing

All universes are parallel—like the cat in the box,
either living or dead but alive

somewhere else or the book on the table like the book
on a table in another realm where a man just like you

stands by a window reviewing the feelings that divide him—
on the one hand, he is happy, on the other, he imagines

a different happiness. In the photo I took
you are walking away from the camera, crossing

a wooden bridge. The water doubles the image.
Who hasn't confused trees with their reflections,

clouds with mountains, trust with doubt. Meaning
is a mirror to memory when we speak

and an echo resounds in an alternate world
where everything is more of the same

and it is common to mistake then for now.
I say mistakes are easy to repeat which is why

I can picture you holding someone else, telling her
the things you swore you'd never tell.

Sea Turtle

A day so hot the water shimmied with heat.
A few miles out, you cut the engine.
A mirage, you said, tipping your hat
to shade your eyes when I pointed
to a far-off shape. I squinted through
midday glare, watching it come closer.
Then she was unmistakable—
brown fist-sized head, beaked nose,
mouth that seemed to smile.
She kept a little distance
as if unsure what moved us
or what creatures could be
cased in so much light.
She followed in our wake
to Lieutenant Island
where we cooled off in the shallows.
The sand stirred with fiddler crabs,
minnows traced our shadows.
You drifted near shore, I swam
close enough to almost touch her—
barnacles specked her carapace,
a yellow crease compassed each eye.
She watched me, unblinking.
Across the bay, our rented house
looked not shingled brown but gilded,
suspended above the narrow stairs
leading to the beach.

In the Balance

It was before we ever thought
to sell the summer house, before days
grew short and time hurried us faster
than we ever knew it could, when summer slowed
whatever was coming next—the daughter leaving
for the wrong man, the wrong man taking
money from her wallet, showing her
the back of his hand, or was it worse than that?
The more she gave, the more he took.

It was before I sat on the dock and read
book after book, looking for daughters in words
others wrote. Around me, birches, hemlocks,
their wavering likenesses. How could I not disturb
the surface when I stepped into the water,
not make it assemble itself again? I thought
one had nothing to do with the other.
But I was starting to understand stealing a heart,
no going back, at the mercy of

"Love," she said. And refused to see the difference.
It was before perch depleted the trout
and we hung baited traps and kept a count.
I counted on the balance. Let everything live
except regret. What would I give up
to get a daughter back? You've heard those stories:
a mother lifting the back of the truck
to free her child pinned under it, the inhuman
strength, the beast in her ready to attack.

More summers would come and go
before we grew too old for the house,
emptied its rooms and didn't look back.
We threw out tangled creels, knots of hooks.
The daughter would finally leave the man.
How do we know what to turn from, how much
to forget? There were summers left
before I thought anything like that.

Bleeding Heart

The garden has its own language
heart's-ease feverfew bishop's weed
wild asters wild roses roses that resist
disease mildew black spot blight

some leaves sicken in the rain
peonies drop their pinks I pluck
shimmering beetles from their green
my granddaughter wants to know the names

each color's shape meaningless
until a word delivers it
into a likeness coral bells
what shines and rings she knows

from picture books but here
are petals spurred like an eagle's claw
clustered like doves columbine
I tell her achillea from the Latin

she likes best the little purses hanging
from their hooks bleeding heart
dicentra from the Latin dis meaning two
on the one hand sorrow on the other love
whether falling in or out of it
whether here now gone
tomorrow time takes us to heart-
break closer than we want

I want only her happiness and pull some
flowers for her outstretched palm
she cups her fingers over them
carefully as if the blood could spill

Pond Road, Truro

Two boys fling their lines where midges swarm
above green plates of lily pads. Late summer heat
defies the change that's coming. Hydrangeas near the porch
are purpling. Past dusk, hemlocks cast longer shadows.

A plaque beside the pond observes the place
pilgrims first drank in the new world.
Up to their knees, indifferent to history, the boys
want to catch something big.

They don't think the season's getting smaller
or crave its return like I do. I have stayed longer than usual
in the rented house, as if buying time
were possible—to purchase back days

when the rooms were filled with family.
But here's what I have come to—the mug of green tea
on the desk, the dog by the kitchen door,
waiting. Not emptiness exactly but a tempering

as if I've been reduced. Who am I
to wish it otherwise—surveyor of cattails,
the boys snagging pond weed, the light
streaming over them. I have leased these extra hours.

They are not mine. I am like those
first settlers crouched in the reeds
not sure where they belong,
though they have reached their destination.

Coming About

The boat moves the water
the way air lifts pages
in the book on the table
by the window. Salt breeze
fills the jib. Coming about,
the boat leans close to the surface;
they almost touch—the real and reflected.
The boat is turning back to the dock.
In a wake of light, the water hurries after.
I was going to say *I love you*
but the day, half-finished
like a story that keeps unfurling,
foreshadows a different ending.
Why else would I put down the book
and wait for you to come through the door?

Daffodils

Some effort of light keeps the dusk unfinished.
Lying on my back, stretching the leg muscle
tight from having bent over the flower beds
planting for a season I can only imagine—
all I see through the skylight is sky
and what moves over it, a v of geese,
a cloud, a leaf. These are all we need
of memory: what passes through the firmament,
what the dead would see looking up
if time made no barrier between coming
and going. My mind keeps the afterimages—
skein of birds, cloud, leaf, what my hands
held before burying. Three hundred bulbs
huddle under the earth,
three hundred odds against weather.
When the darkness takes over,
I close my eyes. Everything is just where I left it.

Editors' Note

Michelle Gillett's original manuscript contained this poem as it appears printed below. We felt some hesitation to remove the passage in lines 8-12 here from the published version on page 3 of this volume, but looking at the poem on its own as well as in the context of the book as a whole, we decided to lean in the direction of deeming the repeated lines a mistake in the typing. While we made small judgments elsewhere, about punctuation for instance, we felt this change was large enough to include here the version presented to us in the original manuscript.

The Lungfish

Deep down inside, I am afraid of the lungfish
suspended in its tank in the darkened room
meant to emulate time when desert was ocean
and ocean was all there was before we crept
on our stubs from the watery hem of existence
and blinked at undiluted light. There was no
going back although we still lacked breath enough
to inherit the earth. Head down in its gloomy tank,
on our stubs from the watery hem of existence
and blinked at undiluted light. There was no
going back although we still lacked breath enough
to inherit the earth. Head down in its gloomy tank,
God's first creature—made in his own image
before we began to feel at home in shallows and muck,
grew legs and arms, sucked in air and named ourselves—
is who we are: bone and gut, God's face before we invented it,
stone-like, wide mouth feeding on every element.

Acknowledgements

Agenda, Bellingham Review, Beloit Poetry Journal, Cape Rock, The Comstock Review, Cortland Review, International Pyschoanalysis, New Mexico Review, Orion, Salamander, Southern Poetry Review, Tupelo Press Poetry Project, and *Upstreet*

The Green Cottage (chapbook)—*The Ledge*

The book's epigraph is from Lucia Berlin's book: A *Manual for Cleaning Women.*

Michelle Gillett was diagnosed with lung cancer in November of 2015 and died four months later on February 11, 2016. Her book, *Coming About*, was selected to be published prior to her death. She lived in Stockbridge, Massachusetts, and was active in the art and literary communities of the Berkshires. Michelle grew up in Hartsdale, New York. She graduated from Skidmore College in 1969 and later graduated from the MFA Program for Writers at Warren Wilson College. In 1980 she was honored as the recipient of the Massachusetts Artists Foundation Poetry Fellowship. Michelle also received the Massachusetts Cultural Council Poetry Finalist Award in 1984, 1987, 1990 and 1994. In 2003, she was awarded the Backwater Press Poetry Book Prize. In addition to writing poetry, Michelle was a columnist for the *Berkshire Eagle* for over thirty years. Her feature columns and opinion columns ranged widely in themes: from gardening and cooking to commentary on current events and worldwide social issues. Michelle spent her life writing and teaching. She was a writing instructor at Austen Riggs, an English teacher at Miss Hall's School and the editor at the *Women's Times*. For the past fifteen years, Michelle taught private writing workshops helping many of her students publish their own work. Michelle is survived by her husband Charles Gillett and her daughters Erin and Lisa Gillett.

Publication of this book was made possible by grants and donations. We are also grateful to those individuals who participated in our 2016 Build a Book Program. They are:

Anonymous (8), Evan Archer, Sally Ball, Jan Bender-Zanoni, Zeke Berman, Kristina Bicher, Carol Blum, Lee Briccetti, Deirdre Brill, Anthony Cappo, Carla & Steven Carlson, Maxwell Dana, Machi Davis, Monica Ferrell, Martha Webster & Robert Fuentes, Dorothy Goldman, Lauri Grossman, Steven Haas, Mary Heilner, Henry Israeli, Christopher Kempf, David Lee, Jen Levitt, Howard Levy, Owen Lewis, Paul Lisicky, Katie Longofono, Cynthia Lowen, Louise Mathias, Nathan McClain, Gregory McDonald, Britt Melewski, Kamilah Aisha Moon, Carolyn Murdoch, Tracey Orick, Zachary Pace, Gregory Pardlo, Allyson Paty, Marcia & Chris Pelletiere, Eileen Pollack, Barbara Preminger, Kevin Prufer, Peter & Jill Schireson, Roni & Richard Schotter, Soraya Shalforoosh, Peggy Shinner, James Snyder & Krista Fragos, Megan Staffel, Marjorie & Lew Tesser, Susan Walton, Calvin Wei, Abigail Wender, Allison Benis White, and Monica Youn.